CHOICE BREAD MACHINE RECIPES COOKBOOK

---

131 DELICIOUS RECIPES FOR 1½ & 2-LB. BREAD MAKERS

KATHERINE HUPP

CONTENTS

INTRODUCTION

Homemade bread is something we all love but rarely have the time to make. Thanks to the bread machine, we can enjoy delicious loaves of warm bread with very little effort at all. The bread machine does the majority of work for us.

This 131 recipe cookbook for the modern bread maker contains delicious recipes created especially for bread machines baking a 1½ to 2-pound loaf. It includes recipes for traditional breads and buns, sweet and savory breads, sourdough and whole grains breads, and even a selection of pizza dough and pretzels.

The majority of the recipes in this cookbook are baked right in the bread machine. All you need to do is add ingredients, select a cooking cycle and enjoy the aroma and taste of homemade, fresh baked bread.

Some recipes will require a little more effort. Most of these are recipes for rolls, buns and pizza dough. Still, the bread machine does most of the work for you. You will simply need to remove the dough from the machine, shape it into the desired form, and let it rise before baking in the oven.

Liquid ingredients are given in ounces rather than cups in the recipes. If a recipe calls for 9 to 11 ounces of liquid, always begin with the lesser amount first. More liquid is added as needed. Humidity and temperature affect how much liquid a bread dough requires, and it is easy to add a little liquid if the dough needs more moisture.

Check the consistency of the dough about 5 minutes after the bread maker begins its first kneading cycle. The dough should form a smooth, supple ball. If it is lumpy, add liquid one tablespoonful at a time. If the dough is sticky, add more flour one tablespoonful at a time.

Even though flour may be added to a recipe, too much flour can impede the rising of the loaf. It is much easier to adjust liquid ingredients than dry ingredients. Be careful not to add too much liquid or the loaf my rise too high and fall. A smooth, supple ball of dough is perfect.

Note that whole grain flours and grains will produce a shorter loaf than all-purpose or bread flours.

Oils may be used to replace butter, margarine or shortening in a recipe. Olive oil produces a softer crust than vegetable oil. Vegetable shortening may also be used and produces a slightly crisper crust.

If a recipe calls for active dry yeast and you want to use bread machine yeast instead, slightly reduce the amount of yeast in the recipe. Using one-half teaspoon of bread machine (quick rising) yeast per cup of flour is a good rule of thumb.

Always use fresh yeast. Old yeast works slowly and is best used in rolls and buns. Allow for additional rising time in the baking pan when working with old yeast.

All-purpose flour containing at least 14% protein may be substituted for bread flour in any recipe.

Try using water that potatoes have been boiled in for an even nicer loaf. Use potato water as a substitution when water is called for in a recipe.

For best results, always begin with ingredients at room temperature unless the recipe instructs otherwise.

TRADITIONAL YEAST BREADS

APPLESAUCE OAT BREAD

4-5 ounces water
¾ cup applesauce, unsweetened
3 tablespoons vegetable oil
1 ½ teaspoons salt
½ cup old-fashioned oats
3 cups bread flour
3 tablespoons white sugar
2 ¼ teaspoons bread machine (fast rise) yeast

Add ingredients to bread maker in the order recommended by the manufacturer. Select the Regular Light setting and press Start.

BASIC BREAD

7-9 ounces water
⅓ cup lukewarm milk
3 tablespoons butter or margarine
1 ½ teaspoons salt
3 ¾ cups all-purpose flour
3 tablespoons white sugar
1 ½ teaspoons bread machine (fast rise) yeast

Add ingredients to bread maker in the order recommended by the manufacturer. Select the Large Loaf/Light Crust or Large Loaf/Dark Crust setting and press Start.

Beer Bread

12 ounces beer, room temperature
1 tablespoon butter or margarine
1 ¼ teaspoons salt
3 ¾ cups all-purpose flour
1 ½ tablespoons white sugar
2 teaspoons bread machine (fast rise) yeast

Add ingredients to bread maker in the order recommended by the manufacturer. Select the Large Loaf/Light Crust or Large Loaf/Dark Crust setting and press Start.

Bread for Toasting

8 ounces lukewarm milk
2 tablespoons butter or margarine
1 ½ teaspoons salt
3 cups all-purpose flour
2 tablespoons sugar
2 teaspoons bread machine (fast rise) yeast

Add ingredients to your bread maker in the order recommended by the manufacturer. Select the Regular Light loaf setting and press Start.

BUTTERMILK BREAD

4-5 ounces lukewarm water
½ cup lukewarm buttermilk
1 teaspoon lemon juice
2 tablespoons butter or margarine
1 teaspoon salt
2 tablespoons brown sugar
3 cups bread flour
2 teaspoons active dry yeast

Add the ingredients to the bread maker in the order recommended by the manufacturer. Select the Regular Light loaf setting and press Start.

CLASSIC WHITE LARGE LOAF

9-11 ounces water
1 ½ teaspoons salt
2 tablespoons butter or margarine
4 cups bread flour
2 tablespoons sugar
2 tablespoons dry milk
2 ¼ teaspoons bread machine (fast rise) dry yeast

Add ingredients to your bread maker in the order recommended by the manufacturer. Select the Large Loaf/Light Crust or Large Loaf/Dark Crust setting and press Start.

CLASSIC WHITE REGULAR LOAF

7-9 ounces water
1 teaspoon salt
1 tablespoons butter or margarine
3 ¼ cups bread flour
1 ½ tablespoons sugar
1 ½ tablespoons dry milk
1 ¾ teaspoons bread machine (fast rise) yeast

Add ingredients to your bread maker in the order recommended by the manufacturer. Select the Regular Light loaf setting and press Start.

COUNTRY WHITE DELUXE LOAF

7-9 ounces milk
1 ½ teaspoons salt
1 large egg
1 ½ tablespoons butter or margarine
4 cups bread flour
3 teaspoons sugar
2 teaspoons active dry yeast

Add the ingredients to the bread pan in the order recommended by the manufacturer. Select the Sweet setting and press Start.

COUNTRY WHITE LARGE LOAF

11-13 ounces water
2 tablespoons butter or margarine
1 ½ teaspoons salt
4 cups bread flour
2 tablespoons non-fat dry milk
2 tablespoons white sugar
2 ¼ teaspoons active dry yeast

Add ingredients to your bread maker in the order recommended by the manufacturer. Select the Large Loaf/Light Crust or Large Loaf/Dark Crust setting and press Start.

COUNTRY WHITE REGULAR LOAF

9-11 ounces water
2 tablespoons butter or margarine
1 ¼ teaspoons salt
3 ⅓ cups bread flour
2 tablespoons non-fat dry milk
1 ½ tablespoons white sugar
2 teaspoons active dry yeast

Add ingredients to your bread maker in the order recommended by the manufacturer. Select the Regular Light loaf setting and press Start.

Deluxe White Large Loaf

10-12 ounces milk
1 ½ teaspoons salt
2 tablespoons butter or margarine
4 cups bread flour
1 ½ tablespoons sugar
2 ¼ teaspoons active dry yeast

Add ingredients to your bread maker in the order recommended by the manufacturer. Select the Large Loaf/Light Crust or Large Loaf/Dark Crust setting and press Start.

Deluxe White Regular Loaf

8-10 ounces milk
1 teaspoon salt
1 ½ tablespoons butter or margarine
3 ¼ cups bread flour
1 tablespoon sugar
1 ¾ teaspoons active dry yeast

Add ingredients to your bread maker in the order recommended by the manufacturer. Select the Regular Light loaf setting and press Start.

Easy Potato Bread

10-11 ounces warm water
2 tablespoons butter or margarine
1 ½ teaspoons salt
3 cups all-purpose flour
½ cup instant dry potato flakes
1 tablespoon sugar
1 ¾ teaspoons bread machine (fast rise) yeast

Add the ingredients to the bread maker in the order recommended by the manufacturer. Select the Regular Light loaf setting and press Start.

EGG BREAD LARGE LOAF

9-10 ounces milk
2 large eggs
2 tablespoons butter or margarine
1 ½ teaspoons salt
4 cups bread flour
2 tablespoons white sugar
2 ¼ teaspoons active dry yeast

Add ingredients to your bread maker in the order recommended by the manufacturer. Select the Large Loaf/Light Crust or Large Loaf/Dark Crust setting and press Start.

EGG BREAD REGULAR LOAF

6-7 ounces milk
2 large eggs
2 tablespoons butter or margarine
1 ¼ teaspoons salt
3 ¼ cups bread flour
1 ½ tablespoons white sugar
2 teaspoons active dry yeast

Add ingredients to your bread maker in the order recommended by the manufacturer. Select the Regular Loaf setting and press Start.

ENGLISH MUFFIN BREAD

1 teaspoon apple cider vinegar
2-3 ounces water
1 cup milk
2 tablespoons vegetable oil
1 ½ teaspoons salt
1 ½ teaspoons white sugar
½ teaspoon baking powder
3 ½ cups all-purpose flour
2 teaspoons bread machine (fast rise) yeast
Cornmeal (optional)

Add ingredients, except cornmeal, to bread maker in the order recommended by the manufacturer. Select the Select the Large Loaf/Light Crust setting and press Start.

Optional: Remove the dough from pan after final kneading and roll in cornmeal. Return to pan in bread maker to complete final rise and baking.

FRENCH BREAD

8-10 ounces water
1 ½ teaspoons salt
2 tablespoons vegetable oil
4 cups bread flour
2 teaspoons sugar
2 teaspoons active dry yeast

Add the ingredients to the bread pan in the order recommended by the manufacturer. Select the French Loaf setting and press Start.

FRENCH BREAD LARGE LOAF

12-13 ounces water
1 ½ tablespoons butter or margarine
1 ½ teaspoons salt
4 ¼ cups bread flour
2 teaspoons sugar
2 ¼ teaspoons active dry yeast

Add the ingredients to the bread pan in the order recommended by the manufacturer. Select the French Loaf setting and press Start.

FRENCH BREAD REGULAR LOAF

10-11 ounces water
1 tablespoon butter or margarine
1 ¼ teaspoons salt
3 ⅓ cups bread flour
1 ½ teaspoons sugar
2 teaspoons active dry yeast

Add the ingredients to the bread pan in the order recommended by the manufacturer. Select the French Loaf setting and press Start.

OATMEAL BREAD LARGE LOAF

9-11 ounces water
1 ½ teaspoons salt
2 tablespoons honey
1 ½ tablespoon butter or margarine
⅔ cup quick cooking oats
3 ¼ cups bread flour
2 teaspoons active dry yeast

Add ingredients to your bread maker in the order recommended by the manufacturer. Select the Large Loaf/Light Crust or Large Loaf/Dark Crust setting and press Start.

OATMEAL BREAD REGULAR LOAF

7-9 ounces water
1 teaspoon salt
1 ½ tablespoons honey
1 tablespoon butter or margarine
½ cups quick cooking oats
2 ½ cups bread flour
1 ¾ teaspoons active dry yeast

Add ingredients to your bread maker in the order recommended by the manufacturer. Select the Regular Light loaf setting and press Start.

POTATO BREAD LARGE LOAF

12-14 ounces water
2 tablespoons butter or margarine
1 ½ teaspoons salt
3 ¾ cups bread flour
⅔ cup instant dry potato flakes
2 tablespoons non-fat dry milk
2 tablespoons white sugar
2 ¼ teaspoons active dry yeast

Add ingredients to your bread maker in the order recommended by the manufacturer. Select the Large Loaf/Light Crust or Large Loaf/Dark Crust setting and press Start.

POTATO BREAD REGULAR LOAF

11-12 ounces water
2 tablespoons butter or margarine
1 ¼ teaspoons salt
3 ¼ cups bread flour
½ cup instant dry potato flakes
2 tablespoons non-fat dry milk
1 ½ tablespoons white sugar
1 ¾ teaspoons active dry yeast

Add ingredients to your bread maker in the order recommended by the manufacturer. Select the Regular Light loaf setting and press Start.

SANDWICH BREAD

10-11 ounces water
1 ¼ tablespoons honey
½ cup dry milk
2 tablespoons butter
1 ½ teaspoons salt
4 cups all-purpose flour
1 ½ teaspoons bread machine (fast rise) yeast

Add ingredients to your bread maker in the order recommended by the manufacturer. Select the Large Loaf/Light Crust or Large Loaf/Dark Crust setting and press Start.

SWEET BUTTER BREAD

4-5 ounces lukewarm water
½ cup lukewarm milk
1 ½ teaspoons salt
1 large egg
5 tablespoons butter
3 ½ cups bread flour
3 tablespoons sugar
2 ¼ teaspoons active dry yeast

Add the ingredients to the bread maker in the order recommended by the manufacturer. Select the Large Loaf/Light Crust setting and press Start.

WHITE SANDWICH BREAD

9-11 ounces water
1 ½ teaspoons salt
1 ½ tablespoons butter
2 tablespoons white sugar
1 ½ tablespoons nonfat dry milk
3 ¾ cups all-purpose flour
1 ½ teaspoons bread machine (fast rise) yeast

Add ingredients to your bread maker in the order recommended by the manufacturer. Select the Large Loaf/Light Crust or Large Loaf/Dark Crust setting and press Start.

SWEET BREADS

APPLE WALNUT BREAD

7-9 ounces unsweetened apple juice
1 teaspoon salt
1 large egg
3 tablespoons butter or margarine
1 large egg
4 cups bread flour
½ cup chopped walnuts
¼ cup brown sugar, packed
1 ¼ teaspoons ground cinnamon
½ teaspoon baking soda
2 teaspoons active dry yeast

Add the ingredients to the bread pan in the order recommended by the manufacturer. Select the Sweet setting and press Start.

ANISE NUT LOAF

6-7 ounces water
1 large egg
¼ cup butter or margarine
½ teaspoon salt
3 cups bread flour
1 teaspoon anise seed
¼ cup sugar
2 teaspoons active dry yeast
½ cup chopped nuts

Place all of the ingredients, except for nuts, into the pan of your bread machine. Select the Regular Light loaf setting and press Start. Add nuts when bread maker sounds signal for adding additional ingredients.

APRICOT ALMOND LOAF

11-12 ounces water
2 tablespoons butter or margarine
1 ½ teaspoon salt
3 ¾ cups bread flour
2 tablespoons non-fat dry milk
3 tablespoons packed dark brown sugar
¾ teaspoon ground nutmeg
2 ¼ teaspoons active dry yeast
⅔ cup dried apricots, chopped
⅓ cup slivered almonds

Place all of the ingredients, except for apricots and almonds, into the pan of your bread machine. Select the Sweet Loaf setting and press Start. Add apricots and almonds when bread maker sounds signal for adding additional ingredients.

BOSTON BROWN BREAD

7-9 ounces buttermilk
1 large egg
¼ cup molasses
2 tablespoons butter or margarine
¾ teaspoon salt
2 ¼ cups bread flour
½ cup whole wheat flour
¼ cup rye flour
1 tablespoon packed dark brown sugar
½ teaspoon baking soda
2 teaspoons active dry yeast
½ cup raisins
⅓ cup slivered almonds

Place all of the ingredients, except for raisins and almonds, into the pan of your bread machine. Select the Sweet Loaf setting and press Start. Add raisins and almonds when bread maker sounds signal for adding additional ingredients.

BUTTERED RUM LOAF

8-9 ounces water
1 large egg
1 tablespoon rum or rum extract
3 tablespoons butter or margarine
3 cups bread flour
1 ¼ teaspoons salt
½ teaspoon ground cinnamon
¼ teaspoon ground nutmeg
¼ teaspoon ground cardamom
3 tablespoons dark brown sugar
2 teaspoons bread machine (fast rise) yeast

Add the ingredients to the bread maker in the order recommended by the manufacturer. Select the Regular Light loaf setting and press Start.

CARAMEL APPLE BREAD

8-9 ounces water
2 tablespoons butter or margarine
1 teaspoon salt
3 cups bread flour
¼ cup packed dark brown sugar
1 ½ teaspoons ground cinnamon
2 teaspoons bread machine (fast rise) yeast
½ cup apple, chopped
⅓ cup pecans, chopped

Place all of the ingredients, except for the apple and nuts, into the pan of your bread machine. Select the Sweet Loaf setting and press Start. Add apple and nuts when bread maker sounds signal for adding additional ingredients.

CARROT RAISIN BREAD

8 ounces water
3 tablespoons mayonnaise
½ cup grated carrots
3 ¼ cups bread flour
3 tablespoons white sugar
1 ½ teaspoons salt
1 ¾ teaspoons bread machine (fast rise) yeast
⅓ cup raisins

Place all of the ingredients, except for the raisins, into the pan of your bread machine. Select the Sweet Loaf setting and press Start. Add raisins when bread maker sounds signal for adding additional ingredients.

CHOCOLATE WALNUT BREAD

11-12 ounces water
1 ½ teaspoons vanilla extract
1 ½ teaspoons salt
3 ½ bread flour
1 ½ teaspoons bread machine (fast rise) yeast
1 teaspoon sugar
½ cup walnuts, chopped
1 cup semi-sweet chocolate chips

Place all of the ingredients, except the chocolate chips and walnuts, into the pan of your bread machine. Select the Sweet Loaf setting and press Start. Add nuts and chocolate when bread maker sounds signal for adding additional ingredients.

CINNAMON CANDIES LOAF

9-10 ounces water
2 teaspoons vanilla extract
1 large egg
3 tablespoons butter or margarine
3 tablespoons nonfat dried milk
1 teaspoon ground cinnamon
1 ½ teaspoons salt
½ teaspoon baking powder
3 tablespoons sugar
4 cups all-purpose flour
1 tablespoon bread machine (fast rise) yeast
1 cup cinnamon candies

Add the ingredients, except for cinnamon candies, to the bread maker in the order recommended by the manufacturer. Select the Select the Large Loaf/Light Crust setting and press Start. Add candies when bread maker sounds signal for adding additional ingredients.

CINNAMON OATMEAL RAISIN LARGE LOAF

12-14 ounces milk
2 tablespoons butter or margarine
1 ½ teaspoons salt
3 ¼ cups bread flour
1 cup quick-cooking oats
2 tablespoons packed brown sugar
1 ¼ teaspoons ground cinnamon
2 teaspoons bread machine (fast rise) yeast
⅔ cup raisins

Place all of the ingredients, except for the raisins, into the pan of your bread machine. Select the Sweet Loaf setting and press Start. Add raisins when bread maker sounds signal for adding additional ingredients.

CINNAMON OATMEAL RAISIN REGULAR LOAF

10-12 ounces milk
2 tablespoons butter or margarine
1 ¼ teaspoons salt
2 ¾ cups bread flour
¾ cup quick-cooking oats
2 tablespoons packed brown sugar
1 teaspoon ground cinnamon
1 ¾ teaspoons bread machine (fast rise) yeast
½ cup raisins

Place all of the ingredients, except for the raisins, into the pan of your bread machine. Select the Sweet Loaf setting and press Start. Add raisins when bread maker sounds signal for adding additional ingredients.

CINNAMON RAISIN BREAD

8-9 ounces water
1 teaspoon vanilla extract
2 tablespoons butter or margarine, room temperature
1 ½ teaspoons salt
3 cups bread flour
3 tablespoons sugar
1 teaspoon ground cinnamon
2 ½ teaspoons bread machine (fast rise) yeast
¾ cup raisins

Place all of the ingredients, except for the raisins, into the pan of your bread machine. Select the Sweet Loaf setting and press Start. Add raisins when bread maker sounds signal for adding additional ingredients.

COFFEE CAKE

Cake
6 ounces milk
1 teaspoons salt
1 egg yolk
1 tablespoon butter or margarine
2 ¼ cups bread flour
¼ cup sugar
2 teaspoons bread machine (fast rise) yeast

Topping
2 tablespoons butter or margarine, melted
½ cup sugar
1 teaspoon ground cinnamon
½ cup chopped pecans

Glaze
½ cup confectioners' sugar
¼ teaspoon vanilla extract
2 teaspoons milk

Place all of the ingredients into the pan of your bread machine in order suggested by manufacturer. Select the Dough setting and press Start. Grease a 9-inch cake pan and set aside.

Remove dough from pan when dough cycle finishes. Pat into prepared cake pan. Cover with plastic wrap or kitchen towel. Set in a warm place and let rise for 30 35 minutes. Drizzle melted butter over dough. In a small bowl, mix sugar, cinnamon and nuts together. Sprinkle topping on butter.

Preheat oven to 375 F. Bake in preheated oven 20-25 minutes. Remove from oven to cool.

In a small bowl, blend confectioners' sugar, vanilla and milk until smooth. Add additional milk or sugar until desired consistency is achieved. Drizzle glaze over slightly warm coffeecake.

Berry & Poppy Seed Loaf

8-9 ounces water
¼ cup butter or margarine, melted
2 large eggs
½ teaspoon lemon oil (optional)
2 ½ cups all-purpose flour
1 cup whole wheat flour
⅓ cup nonfat dry milk
¼ cup poppy seeds
¾ cup dried berries of your choice
1 ½ teaspoons salt
1 ½ teaspoons cardamom
⅓ cup sugar
1 tablespoon bread machine (fast rise) yeast

Add the ingredients to the bread maker in the order recommended by the manufacturer. Select the Large Loaf/Light Crust setting and press Start.

Fruit & Nut Loaf

5-7 ounces orange juice
1 teaspoon salt
1 large egg
1 tablespoons vegetable oil
2 tablespoons apricot jam
3 ½ cups bread flour
¼ teaspoon grated lemon peel
2 teaspoons active dry yeast
¼ cup chopped almonds
¼ cup raisins
¼ cup chopped nuts

Add the ingredients to the bread pan in the order recommended by the manufacturer. Select the Sweet setting and press Start.

JULEKAGE LOAF

1 large egg
8-9 ounces water
½ teaspoon ground cardamom
1 teaspoon salt
1 heaping tablespoon white sugar
¼ cup butter or margarine
3 cups all-purpose flour
1 ¼ teaspoons bread machine (fast rise) yeast
⅓ cup raisins
⅓ cup candied fruit

Place all of the ingredients, except for raisins and candied fruit, into the pan of your bread machine. Select the Sweet Loaf setting and press Start. Add raisins and candied fruit when bread maker sounds signal for adding additional ingredients.

MAPLE PECAN OAT BREAD

7-9 ounces water
⅔ cup maple syrup
2 tablespoons butter or margarine
1 ½ teaspoons salt
2 ½ cups bread flour
¾ cup old fashioned oats
2 tablespoons non-fat dry milk
1 ¾ teaspoons bread machine (fast rise) yeast
½ cup pecans, chopped

Place all of the ingredients, except for pecans, into the pan of your bread machine. Select the Sweet Loaf setting and press Start. Add pecans when bread maker sounds signal for adding additional ingredients.

MEXICAN BUTTERY SWEET BREAD

½ cup lukewarm milk
4-5 ounces lukewarm water
1 large egg
¼ cup unsalted butter
1 teaspoon salt
3 ½ cups bread flour
¼ cup sugar
2 ¼ teaspoons bread machine (fast rise) yeast

Add the ingredients to the bread maker in the order recommended by the manufacturer. Select the Sweet Loaf setting and press Start.

PANETTONE LARGE LOAF

7-9 ounces water
2 large eggs
1 teaspoon vanilla extract
3 tablespoons butter or margarine
2 tablespoons grated lemon peel
4 cups bread flour
1 ½ teaspoons salt
3 tablespoons sugar
2 teaspoons bread machine (fast rise) yeast
½ cup raisins
½ cup candied fruit
3 tablespoons slivered almonds

Place all of the ingredients, except for raisins, candied fruit and almonds, into the pan of your bread machine. Select the Sweet Loaf setting and press Start. Add raisins, candied fruit and almonds when bread maker sounds signal for adding additional ingredients.

PANETTONE REGULAR LOAF

4-5 ounces water
2 large eggs
1 teaspoon vanilla extract
¼ cup butter or margarine
2 tablespoons grated lemon peel
3 cups bread flour
½ teaspoon salt
¼ cup sugar
1 ½ teaspoons bread machine (fast rise) yeast
½ cup raisins
½ cup candied fruit
2 tablespoons slivered almonds

Place all of the ingredients, except for raisins, candied fruit and almonds, into the pan of your bread machine. Select the Sweet Loaf setting and press Start. Add raisins, candied fruit and almonds when bread maker sounds signal for adding additional ingredients.

PINEAPPLE SWEET BREAD

1 ¼ cups warm water
3 tablespoons buttermilk
1 teaspoon salt
4 tablespoons honey
4 tablespoons butter or margarine
4 cups bread flour
½ cup dried pineapple, chopped
2 teaspoons sugar
2 ½ teaspoons bread machine (fast rise) yeast

Add the ingredients to the bread maker in the order recommended by the manufacturer. Select the Sweet Loaf setting and press Start.

Raisin Bran Bread Large Loaf

11-13 ounces water
3 tablespoons honey
1 ½ teaspoons salt
2 tablespoon butter or margarine
2 cups raisin bran cereal
¾ cup raisins
3 ¾ cups bread flour
2 tablespoons dry milk
1 ½ teaspoons ground cinnamon
2 ¼ teaspoons bread machine (fast rise) yeast

Add ingredients to your bread maker in the order recommended by the manufacturer. Select the Large Loaf/Light Crust setting and press Start

Raisin Bran Bread Large Loaf

9-10 ounces water
1 tablespoon honey
1 teaspoon salt
2 tablespoon butter or margarine
1 ½ cups raisin bran cereal
½ cup raisins
2 ⅔ cups bread flour
2 tablespoons dry milk
1 teaspoon ground cinnamon
1 ½ teaspoons bread machine (fast rise) yeast

Add ingredients to your bread maker in the order recommended by the manufacturer. Select the Regular Light loaf setting and press Start.

RAISIN BREAD LARGE LOAF

9-11 ounces water
1 ½ teaspoons salt
2 tablespoon butter or margarine
4 cups bread flour
3 tablcspoons sugar
2 tablespoons dry milk
1 ½ teaspoons cinnamon
2 ¼ teaspoons active dry yeast
1 cup raisins

Add ingredients, except for raisins, to your bread maker in the order recommended by the manufacturer. Select the Large Loaf/Light Crust setting and press Start. Add raisins when bread maker sounds signal for adding additional ingredients.

RAISIN BREAD REGULAR LOAF

7-9 ounces water
1 teaspoon salt
1 ½ tablespoons butter or margarine
3 cups bread flour
2 tablespoons sugar
1 ½ tablespoons dry milk
1 teaspoon cinnamon
1 ¾ teaspoons active dry yeast
¾ cup raisins

Add ingredients to your bread maker, except for raisins, in the order recommended by the manufacturer. Select the Regular Light loaf setting and press Start. Add raisins when bread maker sounds signal for adding additional ingredients.

Rum Raisin Bread

2 tablespoons rum
½ cup raisins
6 ounces warm water
2 tablespoons heavy cream
2 teaspoons butter or margarine
1 teaspoon salt
½ teaspoon rum extract
1 large egg
2 teaspoons brown sugar
3 cups bread flour
2 tablespoons nonfat dry milk
2 teaspoons bread machine (fast rise) yeast

Place rum and raisins in a small bowl and set aside. Add remaining ingredients to bread maker in the order recommended by the manufacturer. Program the machine for Sweet/Fruit setting and press Start. Add rum and raisins when bread maker sounds signal for adding additional ingredients.

Sour Cream & Apricot Bread

4 ounces sour cream
2 large eggs
¾ cup orange juice
¾ cup apricots, chopped
3 ½ cups all-purpose flour
1 ½ teaspoons salt
⅓ cup instant potato flakes
¼ cup sugar
1 tablespoon bread machine (fast rise) yeast

Add the ingredients to the bread maker in the order recommended by the manufacturer. Select the Large Loaf/Light Crust setting and press Start.

SOUR CREAM & VANILLA BREAD

4 ounces water
1 tablespoon vanilla
⅓ cup sour cream
1 large egg
1 tablespoon butter or margarine, room temperature
1 ¼ teaspoons salt
3 cups all-purpose flour
3 tablespoons sugar
2 teaspoons bread machine (fast rise) yeast

Place all of the ingredients, except for the raisins, into the pan of your bread machine. Select the Sweet Loaf setting and press Start. Add raisins when bread maker sounds signal for adding additional ingredients.

SPICED BREAD

6 ounces water
⅓ cup molasses
2 tablespoons butter or margarine
1 teaspoon lemon peel, grate
3 cups bread flour
1 teaspoon salt
1 teaspoon ground ginger
½ teaspoon ground cinnamon
2 teaspoons bread machine (fast rise) yeast

Add the ingredients to the bread maker in the order recommended by the manufacturer. Select the Regular Light loaf setting and press Start.

SPICED WHITE CHOCOLATE BREAD

4 ounces lukewarm milk
4-5 ounces lukewarm water
1 ½ teaspoons vanilla extract
1 ¼ teaspoons salt
2 tablespoons sugar
2 teaspoons ground cinnamon
1 teaspoon ground ginger
2 tablespoons butter or margarine
3 cups bread flour
2 ½ teaspoons bread machine (fast rise) yeast
1 ⅓ cups white chocolate chips

Add the ingredients, except for chocolate chips, to the bread maker in the order recommended by the manufacturer. Select the Select the Regular Light Loaf setting and press Start. Add chocolate when bread maker sounds signal for adding additional ingredients.

STOLLEN LARGE LOAF

8-9 ounces water
2 tablespoons butter or margarine
1 ½ teaspoons salt
4 cups all-purpose flour
3 tablespoons sugar
2 teaspoons bread machine (fast rise) yeast
⅓ cup candied red cherries
⅓ cup candied green cherries
⅓ cup raisins
⅓ cup chopped nuts

Confectioners' sugar for dusting (optional)

Place all of the ingredients, except for cherries, raisins and nuts into the pan of your bread machine. Select the Sweet Loaf setting and press Start. Add cherries, raisins and nuts when bread maker sounds signal for adding additional ingredients.

Remove loaf from pan and allow to cool. Dust loaf with confectioners' sugar, if desired.

STOLLEN REGULAR LOAF

7-8 ounces water
2 tablespoons butter or margarine
1 teaspoons salt
2 ½ cups all-purpose flour
1 ½ tablespoons sugar
1 ¾ teaspoons bread machine (fast rise) yeast
¼ cup candied red cherries
¼ cup candied green cherries
¼ cup raisins
¼ cup chopped nuts

Confectioners' sugar for dusting (optional)

Place all of the ingredients, except for cherries, raisins and nuts into the pan of your bread machine. Select the Sweet Loaf setting and press Start. Add cherries, raisins and nuts when bread maker sounds signal for adding additional ingredients.

Remove loaf from pan and allow to cool. Dust loaf with confectioners' sugar, if desired.

STRAWBERRY RHUBARB LOAF

4 ounces milk
4-5 ounces water
⅓ cup strawberries, chopped
⅓ cup rhubarb, chopped
1 teaspoon salt
3 cups all-purpose flour
2 tablespoons sugar
2 teaspoons bread machine (fast rise) yeast

Add the ingredients to the bread maker in the order recommended by the manufacturer. Select the Large Loaf/Light Crust setting and press Start.

SWEET TURTLE BREAD

8-9 ounces water
½ teaspoon salt
12 caramels, chopped
2 ⅔ cups bread flour
2 tablespoons non-fat dry milk
1 tablespoon brown sugar
1 ½ teaspoons bread machine (fast rise) yeast
¼ cup semisweet chocolate chips
½ cup pecans, chopped

Place all of the ingredients, except for the chocolate chips and nuts, into the pan of your bread machine. Select the Sweet Loaf setting and press Start. Add chocolate chips and nuts when bread maker sounds signal for adding additional ingredients.

WHOLE WHEAT CRANBERRY BREAD

9-10 ounces water
¼ cup honey
2 tablespoons butter or margarine
2 cups all-purpose flour
1 ¼ cups whole wheat flour
1 ½ teaspoons salt
¾ teaspoon ground mace
1 teaspoon sugar
2 teaspoons bread machine (fast rise) yeast
½ cup dried cranberries of golden raisins

Place all of the ingredients, except for cranberries, into the pan of your bread machine. Select the Regular Light loaf setting and press Start. Add cranberries when bread maker sounds signal for adding additional ingredients.

WHOLE WHEAT RAISIN BREAD

9-10 ounces water
¼ cup honey
2 tablespoons butter or margarine
2 cups all-purpose flour
1 ¼ cups whole wheat flour
1 ½ teaspoons salt
¾ teaspoon ground cinnamon
1 teaspoon sugar
2 teaspoons bread machine (fast rise) yeast
½ cup raisins

Place all of the ingredients, except for raisins, into the pan of your bread machine. Select the Regular Light loaf setting and press Start. Add raisins when bread maker sounds signal for adding additional ingredients.

ZUCCHINI BREAD

4 ounces water
1 large egg
2 tablespoons butter or margarine
1 cup shredded zucchini, drained and blotted dry
3 cups bread flour
1 ½ teaspoons salt
½ cup chopped nuts
2 tablespoons non-fat dry milk
2 tablespoons white sugar
1 ½ teaspoons ground cinnamon
½ teaspoon ground cloves
½ teaspoon ground ginger
¼ teaspoon ground nutmeg
1 ½ teaspoons bread machine (fast rise) yeast

Add the ingredients to the bread maker in the order recommended by the manufacturer. Select the Select the Regular Light Loaf setting and press Start.

SAVORY BREADS

ASIAGO TOMATO BREAD

10-11 ounces water
2 tablespoons oil
1 teaspoon lemon juice
1 tablespoon sugar
2 tablespoons powdered milk
1 teaspoon salt
3 cups bread Flour
2 tablespoons sun-dried tomatoes, chopped
¼ cup Asiago cheese, grated
¾ teaspoon dried basil
½ teaspoon black pepper
2 teaspoons bread maker (fast rise) yeast

Add ingredients to your bread maker in the order recommended by the manufacturer. Select the Regular Light loaf setting and press Start.

BUTTERMILK RYE BREAD

7-8 ounces water
1 cup buttermilk
2 tablespoons vegetable oil
1 ¼ teaspoons salt
½ cup instant dry potato flakes
3 cups bread flour
1 ¼ cups rye flour
2 tablespoons molasses
1 ¾ teaspoons caraway seeds
2 ¼ teaspoons bread yeast (fast rise) yeast

Add the ingredients to the bread maker in the order recommended by the manufacturer. Select the Large Loaf/Light Crust setting and press Start.

CARAMELIZED ONION LOAF

Caramelized onions
Peel and slice 2 onions; set aside. In a skillet, melt 1 tablespoon butter over medium-low heat. Add onions and cook 10 to 15 minutes, stirring occasionally. Onions are done when browned and caramelized. Remove from heat.

Bread
8-9 ounces water
1 tablespoon oil
3 cups all-purpose bread flour
2 tablespoons sugar
1 teaspoon salt
2 teaspoons bread machine (fast rise) yeast

Place all of the ingredients, except for caramelized onions, into the pan of your bread machine. Select the Regular Light loaf setting and press Start. Add caramelized onions when bread maker sounds signal for adding additional ingredients.

CHEDDAR CHEESE BREAD

8-9 ounces lukewarm milk
1 tablespoon vegetable oil
3 cups all-purpose flour
1 ¼ teaspoons salt
1 cup grated cheddar cheese   60g
¼ cup grated parmesan cheese   20g
1 tablespoon sugar
1 ¾ teaspoons bread machine (fast rise) yeast

Add the ingredients to the bread pan in the order recommended by the manufacturer. Select the Large Loaf/Light Crust setting and press Start.

CHEESE & ONION BREAD

10-11 ounces water
3 tablespoons non-fat dry milk
1 ½ teaspoons salt
4 cups all-purpose flour
2 tablespoons dried onion flakes
⅓ cup cheddar cheese, shredded
2 tablespoons sugar
1 ¼ teaspoons bread machine (fast rise) yeast

Add the ingredients to the bread maker in the order recommended by the manufacturer. Select the Sweet Loaf setting and press Start.

COTTAGE CHEESE AND CHIVES BREAD

3 ounces water
1 cup cottage cheese
1 large egg
2 tablespoons butter or margarine
1 ½ teaspoons salt
3 ¼ cups bread flour
½ cup fresh chives, chopped or 3 tablespoons dried chives
2 ½ tablespoons white sugar
2 ¼ teaspoons active dry yeast

Add the ingredients to the bread maker in the order recommended by the manufacturer. Select the Sweet Loaf setting and press Start.

CREAM CHEESE & WILD RAMPS BREAD

7-8 ounces lukewarm water
⅓ cup cream cheese, room temperature
1 ½ teaspoons salt
1 tablespoon sugar
3 cups bread flour
½ cup fresh ramp greens, chopped
2 ½ teaspoons bread machine (fast rise) yeast

Add the ingredients to the bread maker in the order recommended by the manufacturer. Select the Select the Regular Light Loaf setting and press Start.

CRUSTY RYE BREAD

1 ½ cups water
3 tablespoons molasses
2 tablespoons vegetable oil
3 teaspoons caraway seed
2 cups bread flour
1 ½ cups rye flour
½ cup plain cornmeal
2 tablespoons vital wheat gluten
2 tablespoon cocoa powder (optional)
2 teaspoons bread machine (fast rise) yeast
1 teaspoon salt

Add the ingredients to the bread maker in the order recommended by the manufacturer. Select the French Loaf setting and press Start.

DILL BREAD LARGE LOAF

11-13 ounces water
2 tablespoons butter or margarine
1 ½ teaspoons salt
4 cups bread flour
1 ½ tablespoons dill seed
2 tablespoons non-fat dry milk
2 ¼ teaspoons active dry yeast

Add the ingredients to the bread pan in the order recommended by the manufacturer. Select the Large Loaf/Light Crust setting and press Start.

DILL BREAD REGULAR LOAF

9-11 ounces water
2 tablespoons butter or margarine
1 ¼ teaspoons salt
3 ⅓ cups bread flour
1 tablespoon dill seed
2 tablespoons non-fat dry milk
2 teaspoons active dry yeast

Add the ingredients to the bread maker in the order recommended by the manufacturer. Select the Regular Light loaf setting and press Start.

FRENCH GARLIC BREAD

8-10 ounces water
1 tablespoon butter or margarine
3 ¼ cups all-purpose flour
1 ¼ teaspoons salt
2 teaspoons green onion tops, chopped
1 ½ teaspoons garlic, minced
1 ½ teaspoons sugar
2 teaspoons active dry yeast

Add the ingredients to the bread maker in the order recommended by the manufacturer. Select the French Loaf setting and press Start.

GARLIC BREAD

8-10 ounces water
1 ½ teaspoon salt
1 tablespoon butter or margarine
3 cups bread flour
1 tablespoons non-fat dry milk
1 tablespoon dried parsley
¾ teaspoon garlic powder
1 tablespoon sugar
2 teaspoons active dry yeast

Add the ingredients to the bread maker in the order recommended by the manufacturer. Select the Regular Light loaf setting and press Start.

GARLIC BREAD LARGE LOAF

12-13 ounces water
2 tablespoons butter or margarine
1 ½ teaspoons salt
4 cups bread flour
2 tablespoons non-fat dry milk
1 ½ tablespoons dried parsley
1 ½ tablespoons white sugar
1 ½ teaspoons garlic powder
2 ¼ teaspoons active dry yeast

Add ingredients to your bread maker in the order recommended by the manufacturer. Select the Large Loaf/Light Crust or Large Loaf/Dark Crust setting and press Start.

GARLIC BREAD REGULAR LOAF

9-11 ounces water
2 tablespoons butter or margarine
1 teaspoon salt
3 ¼ cups bread flour
2 tablespoons non-fat dry milk
1 tablespoon dried parsley flakes
1 tablespoons white sugar
1 teaspoon garlic powder
2 teaspoons active dry yeast

Add ingredients to your bread maker in the order recommended by the manufacturer. Select the Regular Loaf setting and press Start.

GARLIC BREAD LARGE LOAF II

11-13 ounces water
1 ½ teaspoon salt
2 tablespoons butter or margarine
4 cups bread flour
2 tablespoons non-fat dry milk
1 ½ tablespoons dried parsley
1 ¼ teaspoons garlic powder
1 ½ tablespoons sugar
2 ¼ teaspoons active dry yeast

Add the ingredients to the bread pan in the order recommended by the manufacturer. Select the Large Loaf/Light Crust or Large Loaf/Dark Crust setting and press Start.

GARLIC BREAD REGULAR LOAF II

8-10 ounces water
1 ½ teaspoon salt
1 tablespoon butter or margarine
3 cups bread flour
1 tablespoons non-fat dry milk
1 tablespoon dried parsley
¾ teaspoons garlic powder
1 tablespoon sugar
2 teaspoons active dry yeast

Add the ingredients to the bread maker in the order recommended by the manufacturer. Select the Regular Light loaf setting and press Start.

HERB BREAD

2-3 ounces water
1 cup evaporated milk
1 tablespoon vegetable oil
1 ½ teaspoons salt
1 teaspoon celery seed
1 ¼ teaspoon rubber sage
⅛ teaspoon ground ginger
⅛ teaspoon marjoram
3 cups bread flour
⅓ cup plain cornmeal
2 ½ tablespoons sugar
2 ¼ teaspoons active dry yeast

Add the ingredients to the bread maker in the order recommended by the manufacturer. Select the Regular Light loaf setting and press Start.

ITALIAN HERB BREAD

7-9 ounces lukewarm water
1 teaspoon salt
1 ½ teaspoons vegetable oil
3 cups bread flour
¼ cup grated parmesan cheese
1 tablespoon dried parsley
2 teaspoons dry onion flakes
¼ teaspoon dry basil
½ teaspoon garlic powder
2 teaspoons sugar
2 teaspoons active dry yeast

Add the ingredients to the bread pan in the order recommended by the manufacturer. Select the French Loaf setting and press Start.

Oat Pecan Loaf

9-11 ounces water
2 ½ tablespoons butter or margarine
1 ¼ teaspoons salt
3 cups all-purpose flour
½ cup old-fashioned oats
2 tablespoons non-fat dry milk
3 tablespoons sugar
2 teaspoons bread machine (fast rise) yeast
½ cup pecans, chopped

Place all of the ingredients, except for nuts, into the pan of your bread machine. Select the Regular Light loaf setting and press Start. Add nuts when bread maker sounds signal for adding additional ingredients.

Onion Rye Bread

12-13 ounces lukewarm water
1 ½ tablespoons vegetable oil
2 tablespoons molasses
1 ½ teaspoons salt
1 ½ cups rye flour
1 ½ cups bread flour
1 cup whole wheat flour
⅓ cup vital wheat gluten
¼ cup non-fat dry milk
1 tablespoon fennel seeds
1 tablespoon cocoa powder
2 teaspoons dried onion flakes
2 teaspoons bread machine (fast rise) yeast

Add the ingredients to the bread maker in the order recommended by the manufacturer. Select the Whole Wheat setting and press Start.

Parmesan Cheese Bread

8-9 ounces lukewarm milk
1 tablespoon vegetable oil
3 cups all-purpose flour
1 ¼ teaspoons salt
1 tablespoon sugar
1 ¼ cups parmesan cheese, grated
1 ¾ teaspoons bread machine (fast rise) yeast

Add the ingredients to the bread pan in the order recommended by the manufacturer. Select the Large Loaf/Light Crust setting and press Start.

Peanut Butter Bread

7-9 ounces water
½ teaspoon salt
½ cup creamy peanut butter
1 ½ tablespoons honey
2 ¾ cups all-purpose flour
2 tablespoons white sugar
2 ½ teaspoons active dry yeast

Add the ingredients to the bread maker in the order recommended by the manufacturer. Select the Regular Light loaf setting and press Start.

POTATO CHIVE BREAD

6-7 ounces lukewarm water
½ cup buttermilk
3 tablespoons butter or margarine
1 ½ teaspoons salt
3 cups all-purpose flour
½ cup instant dry potato flakes
2 tablespoons dried chives
2 ½ tablespoons sugar
2 ¼ teaspoons active dry yeast

Add the ingredients to the bread maker in the order recommended by the manufacturer. Select the Regular Light loaf setting and press Start.

PUMPERNICKEL BREAD

9-10 ounces water
1 ½ teaspoons salt
⅓ cup dark molasses
2 tablespoons vegetable oil
1 ½ cups bread flour
1 cup rye flour
1 cup whole wheat flour
1 tablespoon vital wheat gluten
3 tablespoons baking cocoa
1 ½ teaspoons instant coffee granules
1 ½ tablespoons caraway seed
2 ¼ teaspoons bread machine (fast rise) yeast

Add the ingredients to the bread maker in the order recommended by the manufacturer. Select the Large Loaf/Dark Crust setting and press Start.

PUMPERNICKEL BREAD LARGE LOAF

4-6 ounces milk
4-6 ounces water
1 ½ teaspoons salt
¼ cup molasses
1 tablespoon butter or margarine
2 ¼ cups bread flour
1 cup rye flour
1 teaspoon onion powder
1 tablespoon cocoa powder
2 ¼ teaspoons active dry yeast

Add ingredients to your bread maker in the order recommended by the manufacturer. Select the Large Loaf/Light Crust or Large Loaf/Dark Crust setting and press Start.

PUMPERNICKEL BREAD REGULAR LOAF

3 ounces milk
3-5 ounces water
1 teaspoon salt
2 tablespoons molasses or honey
½ tablespoon butter or margarine
2 cups bread flour
¾ cup rye flour
½ teaspoon onion powder
½ tablespoon cocoa powder
2 teaspoons active dry yeast

Add ingredients to your bread maker in the order recommended by the manufacturer. Select the Regular Light loaf setting and press Start.

RICOTTA & FRESH CHIVES BREAD

8 ounces lukewarm water
⅓ cup ricotta cheese
1 teaspoon olive oil
1 ½ teaspoons salt
1 tablespoon sugar
3 cups bread flour
½ cup fresh chives, chopped
2 ½ teaspoons bread machine (fast rise) yeast

Add the ingredients to the bread maker in the order recommended by the manufacturer. Select the Select the Regular Light Loaf setting and press Start.

RUSSIAN BREAD

10-11 ounces water
2 ½ tablespoons vegetable oil
1 ½ tablespoons dark molasses
1 ½ tablespoons apple cider vinegar
1 teaspoon salt
1 teaspoon chopped dried onion
2 ½ teaspoons caraway seeds
¼ teaspoon fennel seed
⅔ cup oat bran
1 teaspoon instant coffee granules
2 tablespoons cocoa powder
1 ⅓ cups rye flour
2 cups unbleached all-purpose flour
1 teaspoon sugar
2 ½ teaspoons active dry yeast

Add the ingredients to the bread maker in the order recommended by the manufacturer. Select the Large Loaf/Light Crust setting and press Start.

RYE BREAD

12 ounces lukewarm water
2 tablespoons butter or margarine
1 ½ teaspoons salt
1 cup rye flour
2 ¾ cups bread flour
1 ½ tablespoons vital wheat gluten
⅓ cup brown sugar
2 teaspoons caraway seeds
1 ¾ teaspoons bread machine (fast rise) yeast

Add the ingredients to the bread maker in the order recommended by the manufacturer. Select the Large Loaf/Light Crust setting and press Start.

RYE LARGE LOAF

9-10 ounces water
2 tablespoons buttermilk
1 ½ teaspoons salt
1 ½ tablespoons vegetable oil
2 tablespoons honey or molasses
1 teaspoon white vinegar
3 cups bread flour
1 cup rye flour
1 ½ tablespoons caraway seeds
1 tablespoon vital wheat gluten
2 teaspoons active dry yeast

Add ingredients to your bread maker in the order recommended by the manufacturer. Select the Large Loaf/Light Crust or Large Loaf/Dark Crust setting and press Start.

RYE REGULAR LOAF

7-8 ounces water
1 ½ tablespoons buttermilk
1 teaspoon salt
1 tablespoons vegetable oil
1 ½ tablespoons honey or molasses
½ teaspoon white vinegar
2 cups bread flour
1 cup rye flour
1 tablespoon caraway seeds
1 ½ teaspoons vital wheat gluten
1 ¾ teaspoons active dry yeast

Add ingredients to your bread maker in the order recommended by the manufacturer. Select the Regular Light loaf setting and press Start.

SESAME ONION CHEESE BREAD

4 to 5 ounces water
½ cup milk
⅓ cup onion, diced
½ cup cheddar cheese, grated
1 ½ tablespoons butter or margarine
1 ½ tablespoons white sugar
½ teaspoon salt
1 ½ tablespoons sesame seeds
1 ½ cups bread flour
1 ½ cups whole wheat flour
1 tablespoon vital wheat gluten
1 ½ teaspoons bread machine (fast rise) yeast

Add the ingredients to the bread maker in the order recommended by the manufacturer. Select the Sweet Loaf setting and press Start.

SOUTHWESTERN BREAD

7 ounces water
2 tablespoons vegetable oil
1 cup refried beans (fat-free)
1 teaspoon salt
3 tablespoons sugar
3 cups bread flour
½ cup plain cornmeal
2 teaspoons chili powder
1 tablespoon dried onion flakes
2 ¼ teaspoons active dry yeast

Add ingredients to your bread maker in the order recommended by the manufacturer. Select the Regular Light loaf setting and press Start.

SUNFLOWER OAT BREAD

8-9 ounces water
¼ cup honey
2 tablespoons butter or margarine
3 cups bread flour
½ cup old-fashioned oats
2 tablespoons non-fat dry milk
1 ¼ teaspoons salt
2 ¼ teaspoons bread machine (fast rise) yeast
½ cup sunflower kernels

Place all of the ingredients, except for sunflower kernels, into the pan of your bread machine. Select the Large Loaf/Light Crust setting and press Start. Add sunflower kernels when bread maker sounds signal for adding additional ingredients.

SWISS PEPPER BEER BREAD

8-9 ounces stale beer
2 tablespoons vegetable oil
2 ⅔ cups bread flour
¾ cup rye flour
1 teaspoon salt
2 tablespoons white sugar
½ cup Swiss cheese, grated
1 ½ tablespoons jalapeno peppers, chopped
1 ¾ teaspoons bread machine (fast rise) yeast

Add ingredients to your bread maker in the order recommended by the manufacturer. Select the Regular Light loaf setting and press Start.

TOMATO BASIL RYE BREAD

8 ounces water
2 tablespoons vegetable oil
6 sun dried tomato halves, chopped
1 ½ teaspoons salt
2 ⅓ cups bread flour
2 cups all-purpose flour
1 cup rye flour
2 teaspoons dried basil leaves
1 teaspoon sugar
1 ¾ teaspoons bread machine (fast rise) yeast

Add ingredients to your bread maker in the order recommended by the manufacturer. Select the Regular Light loaf setting and press Start.

TOMATO OLIVE BREAD

1 cup buttermilk
1 large egg
1 teaspoon oil
6 ounces tomato paste
½ cup black olives, drained and chopped
2 cups all-purpose flour
½ cup whole wheat flour
½ cup plain cornmeal
1 teaspoon sugar
1 teaspoon garlic powder
1 teaspoon dried basil
1 teaspoon ground black pepper
¾ teaspoon salt
2 ½ teaspoons bread machine (fast rise) yeast

Add the ingredients to the bread maker in the order recommended by the manufacturer. Select the Quick Bread setting and press Start.

YOGURT RYE LOAF

4-6 ounces lukewarm water
1 ½ teaspoons salt
1 large egg
½ cup plain yogurt
2 tablespoons butter or margarine
2 tablespoons molasses
2 ½ cups bread flour
1 ½ cups rye flour
1 ½ tablespoons caraway seeds
¼ teaspoon baking soda
2 ¼ teaspoons active dry yeast

Add the ingredients to the bread pan in the order recommended by the manufacturer. Select the French Loaf setting and press Start.

BUNS, ROLLS & SPECIALTY BREADS

BUTTER ROLLS

6 ounces milk
2 ounces water
¼ cup butter or margarine, softened
1 teaspoon salt
1 large egg, room temperature
2 ¾ cups bread flour
2 tablespoons sugar
2 teaspoons active dry yeast

Add ingredients to your bread maker in the order recommended by the manufacturer. Select the Dough setting and press Start.

Remove dough from pan when dough cycle finishes and turn onto a lightly oiled surface. Shape into a ball and grease with shortening or oil; cover with plastic wrap or kitchen towel. Let rest 10 minutes.

Divide the dough into 12 equal pieces and shape into rolls as desired. Place on greased baking sheet and cover with a towel. Set in a warm location to rise for 30 minutes.

Set oven to 375° F to preheat. Remove covering from rolls and place in preheated oven. Bake for 18 to 20 minutes until lightly browned.

BUTTERY BATTER PAN ROLLS

4-5 ounces water
4 ounces milk
½ teaspoon salt
1 large egg
3 tablespoons butter or margarine
2 cups all-purpose flour
2 tablespoons sugar
2 teaspoons active dry yeast

5 tablespoons butter or margarine, reserved

Add ingredients, except for reserved butter, to your bread maker in the order recommended by the manufacturer. Select the Dough setting and press Start. Remove dough from pan when dough cycle finishes.

Melt reserved butter and pour half into an 8-inch baking pan, being sure to coat entire bottom of pan.

Drop batter by rounded spoonful's into pan, forming 12 to 16 rolls. Pour remaining melted butter over rolls. Cover with plastic wrap or a towel. Set in a warm location to rise for 30 minutes.

Preheat oven to 400° F. Remove covering from rolls and place in preheated oven. Bake for 12-15 minutes or until lightly browned.

CINNAMON ROLLS

Rolls
6-7 ounces water
1 large egg
2 teaspoons vanilla extract
¼ cup softened butter
3 cups all-purpose flour
1 teaspoon salt
2 tablespoons non-fat dry milk
6 tablespoons sugar
1 ¾ teaspoons active dry yeast

Filling
¼ cup butter, melted
⅓ cup brown sugar
1 teaspoon cinnamon
½ cup raisins

Icing
3 tablespoons butter or margarine
1 teaspoon vanilla extract
3 tablespoons hot tap water
2 cups confectioners' sugar

Add ingredients for rolls to your bread maker in the order recommended by the manufacturer. Select the Dough setting and press Start. Remove dough from pan when dough cycle finishes and turn onto lightly floured surface. Roll out to form a 10x18-inch rectangle.

Begin filling by brushing with melted butter. In a small bowl, mix together brown sugar and cinnamon. Spread over melted butter and sprinkle with raisins. Starting at long side, roll up and pinch seams together like a jelly roll. Cut into 12 equal slices. Place rolls cut side up on a greased baking sheet. Cover with plastic wrap or kitchen towel and let rise in a warm place for 50-60 minutes.

Preheat oven to 375° F. Remove covering from rolls and place in preheated oven. Bake for 15 minutes or until lightly browned.

Melt butter in a saucepan over medium heat. Add hot water and vanilla. Remove from heat and stir in confectioners' sugar. Thin with ½ teaspoon hot water if needed. Drizzle over cinnamon rolls.

HONEY & WHEAT ROLLS

8 ounces water
1 teaspoon salt
¼ cup honey
1 large egg
2 cups bread flour
1 cup whole wheat flour
2 teaspoons active dry yeast

Add the ingredients to the bread pan in the order recommended by the manufacturer. Select the Dough setting and press Start. Remove dough from pan when dough cycle finishes and turn onto a lightly oiled surface. Shape into a ball and grease with shortening or oil; cover with plastic wrap or kitchen towel. Let rest 15 minutes.

Divide the dough into 12 equal pieces and shape into rolls as desired. Place on greased baking sheet and cover with a towel. Set in a warm location to rise for 30-45 minutes.

Set oven to 375° F to preheat. Remove covering from rolls and place in preheated oven. Bake for 18 to 20 minutes until lightly browned.

HOT CROSS BUNS

Buns
6 ounces lukewarm water
1 tablespoon nonfat dry milk
3 tablespoons butter or margarine, cut into small pieces
1 large egg
1 egg white
1 teaspoon vanilla extract
1 teaspoon almond extract
½ teaspoon salt
¼ cup white sugar
1 teaspoon ground cinnamon
½ teaspoon ground allspice
¼ teaspoon ground cloves
¾ cup raisins
3 cups all-purpose flour
1 tablespoon bread machine (fast rise) yeast

Glaze
1 egg yolk
2 tablespoons water

Icing
1/2 cup confectioners' sugar
1/4 teaspoon vanilla extract
2 teaspoons milk

Add ingredients for buns to your bread maker in the order recommended by the manufacturer. Select the Dough setting and press Start. Remove dough from pan when dough cycle finishes and turn onto lightly floured surface. Cover with kitchen towel and let rest for 10-15 minutes.

Grease a 9x13-inch baking pan. Separate dough into 12 equal pieces; roll into balls and place in baking pan. Cover with plastic wrap or kitchen towel and let rise in a warm place for 50-60 minutes.

Make egg wash by mixing egg yolk and water together in a small bowl. Remove covering from buns and brush egg wash over buns.

Preheat oven to 375° F. Place buns in preheated oven and bake for 20 minutes or until golden brown. Remove from oven and allow to cool completely before decorating with icing.

In a small bowl, blend confectioners' sugar, vanilla and milk until smooth. Add additional milk or sugar until desired consistency is achieved. Brush or pipe an X on each cooled bun.

ITALIAN BRAIDED BREAD

Starter (Start the night before)
¾ cup all-purpose flour
½ cup warm tap water
⅛ teaspoon bread machine (fast rise) yeast

Dough
2 teaspoons bread machine (fast rise) yeast
⅔ cup water
2 ¾ cups all-purpose flour
1 ¼ teaspoons salt

Glaze
1 egg white
1 tablespoon water
¼ cup sesame seeds

Starter must rest overnight: Mix 3/4 cup all-purpose flour, ½ cup warm tap water and ⅛ teaspoon bread machine yeast in a small bowl. Cover and let rest overnight at room temperature.

Following day: Place all ingredients, including the starter, into bread maker. Select the Dough setting and press Start. After dough cycle finishes, remove the pan from machine, punch dough down slightly and cover pan with a cloth towel. Place pan in a warm area; allow to rest for 30 minutes.

Next, remove dough from pan and transfer to a lightly greased work surface. Divide dough into 3 even sections. With your hands, roll each section back and forth until it resembles an 18-inch long rope. Braid the three lengths together, working over and under; tuck ends underneath to form a neat braid. Place on a lightly greased baking sheet and cover with a towel. Place in a warm area and let rise until braid is puffed up, approximately 1 to 1 ½ hours.

In a small bowl, beat egg white and water. Brush entire upper surface of bread braid with egg wash. Immediately sprinkle generously with sesame seeds. Bake the bread in a preheated 400°F oven for 25 to 35 minutes. Remove from oven and place on a wire rack to cool.

ITALIAN BREAD

Dough
4 cups all-purpose flour
¼ cup dry instant mashed potato flakes
¼ cup nonfat dry milk
2 teaspoons salt
2 teaspoons white sugar
2 teaspoons bread machine (fast rise) yeast
10-11 ounces hot tap water
3 tablespoons olive oil

Glaze
1 egg white
1 tablespoon water
¼ cup sesame seeds

Lightly grease an Italian bread pan or large baking sheet and set aside.

Add dough ingredients to your bread maker in the order recommended by the manufacturer. Select the Dough setting and press Start.

When cycle completes, move dough to a large, greased bowl. Turn dough over so it is greased on all sides. Cover with a towel, place in a warm area and let dough rise for 1 hour, or until double in size.

Remove dough from pan and transfer to a lightly greased work surface. Divide dough into 2 even pieces. With your hands, shape each section to resemble a 16-inch long log. Place dough logs into two spaces of prepared Italian bread pan, or arrange on prepared baking sheet, leaving room between loaves for rising without touching. Cover with a towel, place in a warm area and let rise for 1 hour.

In a small bowl, beat egg white and water. Brush both loaves with egg wash. Immediately sprinkle generously with sesame seeds. With a sharp serrated knife, make 3 or 4 diagonal slashes in each loaf.

Place in preheated 400° F oven and bake for 25 minutes, or until loaves are golden brown. Turn oven off, prop oven door open and allow loaves to cool in oven for a crispy crust.

PUMPKIN & PECAN CINNAMON BUNS

Buns
2-3 ounces lukewarm water
1 cup lukewarm milk
1 cup canned pumpkin
2 eggs
4 tablespoons butter
¼ cup white sugar
¾ teaspoon salt
4 cups bread flour
2 ¼ teaspoons active dry yeast
1 teaspoon ground cinnamon

Filling
½ cup butter or margarine, melted (for spreading)
½ cup packed brown sugar
3 teaspoons ground cinnamon
½ cup coarsely chopped pecans

Icing
1 cup confectioners' sugar
½ teaspoon vanilla extract
4 teaspoons milk
½ teaspoon ground cinnamon
¼ cup finely chopped pecans

Add ingredients for buns to your bread maker in the order recommended by the manufacturer. Select the Dough setting and press Start.

Grease a large baking sheet and set aside.

Remove dough from pan when dough cycle finishes and turn onto lightly floured surface. Roll out to form a 12x18-inch rectangle. Brush dough with melted butter.

In a small bowl, mix together brown sugar and cinnamon; spread over butter. Sprinkle with pecans. Starting at shortest side, roll up dough. Cut into 12 equal slices. Place rolls cut side up on prepared baking sheet. Cover with plastic wrap or kitchen towel and let rise in a warm place for 45-60 minutes.

Preheat oven to 350° F. Remove covering from buns and bake 15 to 20 minutes or until lightly browned. Remove from oven.

In a small bowl, mix together confectioners' sugar, vanilla, milk and cinnamon. Add additional milk or sugar until thick consistency is reached.

Brush icing on buns while buns are still warm. Sprinkle with pecans. Allow buns to cool and icing to set before serving.

SANDWICH BUNS

2-3 ounces lukewarm water
1 cup lukewarm milk
1 large egg
2 tablespoons butter or margarine
¼ cup sugar
¾ teaspoon salt
3 ¾ cups bread flour
1 ¾ teaspoons bread machine (fast rise) yeast
1 tablespoon butter or margarine, melted

Add all ingredients except for melted butter to your bread maker in the order recommended by the manufacturer. Select the Dough setting and press Start. Grease a large baking sheet and set aside.

Remove dough from pan when dough cycle finishes and turn onto lightly floured surface. Divide dough in half and roll each half to a ¾-inch thickness. Cut into 18 buns using a 2 ½-inch round biscuit cutter. Place on prepared baking sheet. Brush tops with melted butter. Cover with plastic wrap or kitchen towel and let rise in a warm place for 50-60 minutes.

Preheat oven to 350° F. Remove covering from buns and bake 10 to 15 minutes until lightly browned.

STICKY BUNS

Buns
2-3 ounces water
1 cup milk
1 teaspoon vanilla extract
3 tablespoons buttcr or margarine
1 teaspoon salt
3 cups all-purpose flour
3 tablespoons white sugar
2 teaspoons bread machine (fast rise) yeast

Filling
6 tablespoons butter or margarine, softened (for spreading)
¾ cup brown sugar
1 tablespoon cinnamon

Topping
⅓ cup butter
1 cup brown sugar
¼ cup light corn syrup
1 cup pecans, coarsely chopped

Add ingredients for buns to your bread maker in the order recommended by the manufacturer. Select the Dough setting and press Start.

Remove dough from pan when dough cycle finishes and turn onto lightly floured surface. Roll out to form a 10x18-inch rectangle.

Spread the 6 tablespoons of softened butter over dough, leaving a bare edge all the way around to make pinching the dough closed easier.

Mix together ¾ cup brown sugar and 1 tablespoon cinnamon; spread over buttered surface of buns.

Starting at long side, roll up and pinch seams together like a jelly roll. Cut into 12 equal slices. Generously grease the bottom and sides of a 13x9x2-inch glass baking dish.

In a small saucepan, heat and stir topping ingredients until brown sugar is dissolved. Pour into prepared baking dish and spread evenly over bottom.

Place buns cut side up in bottom of baking dish, sides touching. Cover with plastic wrap and let rise in a warm place for 45-60 minutes.

Preheat oven to 350° F. Remove covering from buns and place in preheated oven. Bake for 30 minutes or until lightly browned. Remove from oven.

Place a 13x9-inch baking pan upside down over top of baking dish. Hold tightly together and flip over quickly. Caution: Flip as quickly as possible to help keep hot topping from dripping from between pans. Cool slightly before serving.

SWEET BUTTER ROLLS

8-9 ounces lukewarm milk
½ cup butter or margarine, softened
2 eggs, room temperature
¾ teaspoon salt
4 cups bread flour
¼ cup sugar
2 ¾ teaspoons bread machine (fast rise) yeast

Add ingredients to your bread maker in the order recommended by the manufacturer. Select the Dough setting and press Start.
Remove dough from pan when dough cycle finishes and turn onto a lightly oiled surface. Shape into a ball and grease with shortening or oil; cover with plastic wrap or kitchen towel. Let rest 10 minutes.

Divide the dough into 16 equal pieces and shape into rolls as desired. Place on greased baking sheet and cover with a towel. Set in a warm location to rise for 30 minutes.

Set oven to 375° F to preheat. Remove covering from rolls and place in preheated oven. Bake for 18 to 20 minutes until lightly browned.

Pizza Crust & Pretzels

Beer Pretzels

8 ounces stale beer
¼ teaspoon salt
2 ¼ cups all-purpose flour
½ teaspoon sugar
1 ½ teaspoons active dry yeast
1 egg, beaten
1 tablespoon coarse salt

Add all ingredients to bread pan except for egg and coarse salt. Select the Dough setting and press Start.
Remove dough from pan when dough cycle finishes and divide into 12 pieces.

Preheat oven to 450° F. Roll each piece into an 8-inch rope and form into a pretzel shape or leave as pretzel stick.

Place on a greased baking sheet. Brush each pretzel with beaten egg. Sprinkle lightly with coarse salt. Bake for 12-15 minutes in preheated oven.

BREAD PRETZELS

6 ounces water
¼ teaspoon salt
2 cups bread flour
½ teaspoon sugar
1 ½ teaspoons active dry yeast
1 egg, beaten
1 tablespoon coarse salt

Add all ingredients to bread pan except for egg and coarse salt. Select the Dough setting and press Start.
Remove dough from pan when dough cycle finishes and divide into 12 pieces.

Preheat oven to 450° F. Roll each piece into an 8-inch rope and form into a pretzel shape or leave as pretzel stick.

Place on a greased baking sheet. Brush each pretzel with beaten egg. Sprinkle lightly with coarse salt. Bake for 12-15 minutes in preheated oven.

PIZZA CRUST

6 ounces plus 2 tablespoons water
½ teaspoon salt
2 tablespoons vegetable oil
2 ½ cups all-purpose flour
2 teaspoons sugar
2 teaspoons active dry yeast

Add the ingredients to the bread pan in the order recommended by the manufacturer. Select the Dough setting and press Start. Remove from pan when dough cycle finishes and pat into shape for your favorite pizza. Let stand 10 minutes.

Preheat oven to 400° F. Bake pizza 15-20 minutes in preheated oven until crust is golden brown.

Sourdough Pizza Crust

1 cup sourdough starter
½ cup hot tap water
2 ½ cups all-purpose flour
1 teaspoon salt
½ teaspoon bread machine (fast rise) yeast

Add dough ingredients to your bread maker in the order recommended by the manufacturer. Select the Dough setting and press Start.

When cycle completes, divide dough into 2 equal sections and place on 2 greased 12-inch pizza pans. Cover with a towel and let rest for 15 minutes. Using your hands, press dough evenly toward the edges of the pans. Cover and let rest another 15 minutes. Press dough toward edges of pan again, if necessary.

Place in preheated 450° F oven and bake for 5 minutes. Remove from oven, cover with toppings and return to oven. Bake for an additional 8 to 10 minutes until toppings are done.

For thick crust pizza, use a single 14-inch pan and bake at 450° F 12 to 14 minutes during second bake time.

Whole Wheat Pizza Crust

8 ounces water
½ teaspoon salt
1 tablespoon vegetable oil
1 tablespoon honey
2 ¼ cups whole wheat flour
¼ cup wheat germ
2 ¼ teaspoons active dry yeast

Add the ingredients to the bread pan in the order recommended by the manufacturer. Select the Dough setting and press Start. Remove from pan when dough cycle finishes and pat into shape for your favorite pizza. Let stand 10 minutes.

Preheat oven to 400° F. Bake pizza 15-20 minutes in preheated oven until crust is golden brown.

WHOLE GRAIN BREADS

100% WHOLE WHEAT BREAD

11-12 ounces lukewarm water
2 tablespoons vegetable oil
¼ cup honey
3 ½ cups whole wheat flour
1 tablespoon vital wheat gluten
1 ½ teaspoons salt
1 ½ teaspoons bread machine (fast rise) yeast

Add the ingredients to the bread pan in the order recommended by the manufacturer. Select the Whole Wheat setting and press Start.

100% WHOLE WHEAT BREAD II

9-11 ounces water
1 ½ teaspoons salt
1 ½ teaspoons honey
1 ½ teaspoons molasses
3 ½ cups whole wheat flour
1 tablespoon vital wheat gluten
2 teaspoons active dry yeast

Add the ingredients to the bread pan in the order recommended by the manufacturer. Select the Whole Wheat setting and press Start.

100% WHOLE WHEAT BREAD III

10-12 ounces lukewarm water
2 teaspoons salt
2 tablespoons molasses
1 tablespoon brown sugar, packed
4 cups whole wheat flour
1 ½ teaspoons vital wheat gluten
2 teaspoons active dry yeast

Add the ingredients to the bread pan in the order recommended by the manufacturer. Select the Whole Wheat setting and press Start.

BUCKWHEAT WHEAT BREAD

8-9 ounces water
1 tablespoon oil
1 tablespoon honey
1 teaspoon salt
¼ cup non-fat dry milk
2 cups bread flour
½ cup whole wheat flour
¼ cup buckwheat flour
2 tablespoons ground flax seed
2 tablespoons wheat germ
1 tablespoon instant potato flakes
½ teaspoon sugar
1 ¼ teaspoons active dry yeast

Add the ingredients to the bread maker in the order recommended by the manufacturer. Select the French Loaf setting and press Start.

BUTTERMILK WHEAT BREAD

12-13 ounces buttermilk
1 ½ tablespoons butter or margarine
1 teaspoon salt
3 cups bread flour
1 ⅓ cups whole wheat flour
2 tablespoons white sugar
2 ¼ teaspoons active dry yeast

Add the ingredients to the bread maker in the order recommended by the manufacturer. Select the Large Loaf/Dark Crust setting and press Start.

CRACKED WHEAT LARGE LOAF

9-11 ounces water
1 ½ teaspoons salt
1 ½ tablespoons butter or margarine
2 tablespoons honey
2 ¼ cups bread flour
1 ¼ cups whole wheat flour
½ cup cracked wheat
2 ¼ teaspoons active dry yeast

Add ingredients to your bread maker in the order recommended by the manufacturer. Select the Large Loaf/Light Crust or Large Loaf/Dark Crust setting and press Start.

CRACKED WHEAT REGULAR LOAF

7-9 ounces water
1 teaspoon salt
2 teaspoons butter or margarine
1 ½ tablespoons honey
2 cups bread flour
1 cup whole wheat flour
⅓ cup cracked wheat
1 ¾ teaspoons active dry yeast

Add ingredients to your bread maker in the order recommended by the manufacturer. Select the Regular Light loaf setting and press Start.

CRANBERRY PECAN WHEAT BREAD

9-11 ounces water
2 tablespoons butter
1 ¼ teaspoons salt
2 cups bread flour
1 cup whole wheat flour
3 tablespoons brown sugar
2 teaspoons bread machine (fast rise) yeast
1 cup chopped pecans or walnuts
⅔ cup dried cranberries

Add ingredients, except for nuts and cranberries, to bread maker in the order recommended by the manufacturer. Select the Select the Large Loaf/Light Crust setting and press Start.

Add nuts and cranberries when bread maker sounds signal for adding additional ingredients.

HONEY GRAIN LARGE LOAF

9-11 ounces water
1 ½ teaspoons salt
2 ½ tablespoon butter or margarine
2 tablespoons honey
2 ½ cups bread flour
1 ½ cups whole wheat flour
⅔ cups quick cooking oats
2 ¼ teaspoons active dry yeast

Add ingredients to your bread maker in the order recommended by the manufacturer. Select the Large Loaf/Light Crust or Large Loaf/Dark Crust setting and press Start.

HONEY GRAIN REGULAR LOAF

7-9 ounces water
1 teaspoon salt
2 tablespoons butter or margarine
1 ½ tablespoons honey
2 ¼ cups bread flour
1 ¼ cups whole wheat flour
½ cups quick cooking oats
2 teaspoons active dry yeast

Add ingredients to your bread maker in the order recommended by the manufacturer. Select the Regular Light loaf setting and press Start.

HONEY WHEAT LARGE LOAF

1 cup wheat flakes
2 tablespoons wheat bran
7-9 ounces water
1 ¼ teaspoons salt
3 tablespoons honey
1 ½ tablespoons butter or margarine
3 ½ cups bread flour
2 ¼ teaspoons active dry yeast

Add ingredients to your bread maker in the order recommended by the manufacturer. Select the Large Loaf/Light Crust or Large Loaf/Dark Crust setting and press Start.

HONEY WHEAT REGULAR LOAF

6-8 ounces water
¾ cup wheat flakes
1 ½ tablespoons wheat bran
1 teaspoon salt
2 tablespoons honey
1 tablespoons butter or margarine
2 ¾ cups bread flour
1 ¾ teaspoons active dry yeast

Add ingredients to your bread maker in the order recommended by the manufacturer. Select the Regular Light loaf setting and press Start.

MULTI-GRAIN BREAD

¾ cup lukewarm milk
½ cup lukewarm water
2 tablespoons vegetable oil
1 ½ tablespoons honey
2 tablespoons raisins
2 tablespoons brown sugar
1 ½ cups bread flour
1 ¼ cups whole wheat flour
¾ cup rye flour
1 ½ teaspoons salt
2 teaspoons bread machine (fast rise) yeast

First add milk, water, oil, honey, raisins and sugar to pan of bread maker; stir. Add remaining ingredients. Select the Large Loaf/Light Crust setting and press Start.

MULTI-GRAIN FRENCH BREAD

11-13 ounces water
1 ½ tablespoons butter or margarine
2 tablespoons brown sugar
1 ½ teaspoons salt
3 cups bread flour
1 cup whole wheat flour
½ cup 7 grain cereal
2 ¼ teaspoons active dry yeast

Add ingredients to your bread maker in the order recommended by the manufacturer. Select the French loaf setting and press Start.

ONION RYE BREAD

12-13 ounces lukewarm water
1 ½ tablespoons vegetable oil
2 tablespoons molasses
1 ½ teaspoons salt
1 ½ cups rye flour
1 ½ cups bread flour
1 cup whole wheat flour
⅓ cup vital wheat gluten
¼ cup non-fat dry milk
1 tablespoon fennel seeds
1 tablespoon cocoa powder
2 teaspoons chopped dried onion
2 teaspoons bread machine (fast rise) yeast

Add the ingredients to the bread maker in the order recommended by the manufacturer. Select the Whole Wheat setting and press Start.

ORANGE WHEAT BREAD

5-6 ounces water
4 ounces orange juice
2 tablespoons butter or margarine
1 ½ teaspoons salt
1 cup bread flour
2 cups whole wheat flour
¼ cup wheat germ
2 tablespoons grated orange peel
2 tablespoons white sugar
1 tablespoons non-fat dry milk
1 ¾ teaspoons bread machine (fast rise) yeast

Add the ingredients to the bread maker in the order recommended by the manufacturer. Select the Whole Wheat setting and press Start.

PUMPERNICKEL RYE LARGE LOAF

11-13 ounces water
2 tablespoons molasses
3 tablespoons butter or margarine
1 ½ teaspoons salt
2 ⅔ cups bread flour
⅔ cup rye flour
⅔ cup whole wheat flour
2½ tablespoons unsweetened cocoa powder
2 ¼ teaspoons active dry yeast

Add the ingredients to the bread maker in the order recommended by the manufacturer. Select the Whole Wheat setting and press Start.

PUMPERNICKEL RYE REGULAR LOAF

9-11 ounces water
2 tablespoons molasses
3 tablespoons butter or margarine
1¼ teaspoons salt
2¼ cups bread flour
½ cup rye flour
½ cup whole wheat flour
2 tablespoons unsweetened cocoa powder
2 teaspoons active dry yeast

Add the ingredients to the bread maker in the order recommended by the manufacturer. Select the Regular Light setting and press Start.

Sourdough Wheat Large Loaf

6 ounces water
1 ¼ cups sourdough starter
1 tablespoon molasses
1 ¾ cups bread flour
1 ¾ cups whole wheat flour
1 ½ teaspoons salt
2 teaspoon bread machine (fast rise) yeast

Add the ingredients to the bread maker in the order recommended by the manufacturer. Select the Large Loaf/Light Crust setting and press Start.

Sourdough Wheat Regular Loaf

6 ounces water
1 cup sourdough starter
1 tablespoon molasses
1 ½ cups bread flour
1 ½ cups whole wheat flour
1 teaspoons salt
1 ¾ teaspoons bread machine (fast rise) yeast

Add the ingredients to the bread maker in the order recommended by the manufacturer. Select the Regular Light setting and press Start.

STANDARD WHEAT LOAF

8-10 ounces water
1 ½ teaspoons salt
1 ½ tablespoon vegetable oil
2 tablespoons molasses
2 cups bread flour
2 cups whole wheat flour
2 teaspoons active dry yeast

Add ingredients to your bread maker in the order recommended by the manufacturer. Select the Whole Wheat setting and press Start.

SUNFLOWER OATMEAL WHEAT BREAD

9-10 ounces lukewarm water
3 tablespoons honey
2 tablespoons butter or margarine
1 teaspoon salt
1 cup bread flour
2 cups whole wheat flour
⅓ cup quick cooking oats
⅓ cup salted sunflower seeds
1 ½ teaspoons bread machine (fast rise) yeast

Add ingredients to your bread maker in the order recommended by the manufacturer. Select the Whole Wheat setting and press Start.

WHOLE WHEAT CRANBERRY BREAD

9-10 ounces water
¼ cup honey
2 tablespoons butter or margarine
2 cups all-purpose flour
1 ¼ cups whole wheat flour
1 ½ teaspoons salt
¾ teaspoon ground mace
1 teaspoon sugar
2 teaspoons bread machine (fast rise) yeast
½ cup dried cranberries of golden raisins

Place all of the ingredients, except for cranberries, into the pan of your bread machine. Select the Regular Light loaf setting and press Start. Add cranberries when bread maker sounds signal for adding additional ingredients.

WHOLE WHEAT PIZZA CRUST

8 ounces water
½ teaspoon salt
1 tablespoon vegetable oil
1 tablespoon honey
2 ¼ cups whole wheat flour
¼ cup wheat germ
2 ¼ teaspoons active dry yeast

Add the ingredients to the bread pan in the order recommended by the manufacturer. Select the Dough setting and press Start. Remove from pan when dough cycle finishes and pat into shape for your favorite pizza. Let stand 10 minutes.

Preheat oven to 400° F. Bake pizza 15-20 minutes in preheated oven until crust is golden brown.

WHOLE WHEAT RAISIN BREAD

9-10 ounces water
¼ cup honey
2 tablespoons butter or margarine
2 cups all-purpose flour
1 ¼ cups whole wheat flour
1 ½ teaspoons salt
¾ teaspoon ground cinnamon
1 teaspoon sugar
2 teaspoons bread machine (fast rise) yeast
½ cup raisins

Place all of the ingredients, except for raisins, into the pan of your bread machine. Select the Regular Light loaf setting and press Start. Add raisins when bread maker sounds signal for adding additional ingredients.

Quick Breads

Apricot Nut Bread

6 ounces orange juice
1 large egg
2 tablespoons butter or margarine
2 cups all-purpose flour
¾ cup sugar
2 teaspoons baking powder
¼ teaspoon baking soda
1 teaspoon salt
1 cup chopped dried apricots
¾ cup slivered almonds

Add orange juice, egg and butter to the bread pan and set aside. Mix together remaining ingredients in a medium mixing bowl; add to bread pan. Select the Quick Bread setting and press Start.

Banana Bread

2 large eggs
⅓ cup butter or margarine, cut into pieces and softened
1 ounce milk
2 medium bananas, mashed
1 ⅓ cups bread flour
⅔ cup sugar
½ teaspoon baking soda
½ teaspoon salt
½ cup chopped nuts

Add eggs, butter, milk and mashed bananas to bread pan. In a medium bowl, stir dry ingredients together. Add to bread pan. Select the Quick Bread setting and press Start.

BANANA NUT BREAD

2 ounces milk
½ cup butter, cut into pieces and softened
2 large eggs
2 medium bananas, mashed
2 ½ cups all purpose flour
1 cup white sugar
2 ½ teaspoons baking powder
½ teaspoon baking soda
1 teaspoon salt
½ cup chopped nuts

Add eggs, butter, milk and mashed bananas to bread pan. In a medium bowl, stir dry ingredients together. Add to bread pan. Select the Quick Bread setting and press Start.

CHERRY NUT BREAD

10 ounces milk
1 large egg
3 tablespoons vegetable oil
2 ½ cups all-purpose flour
¾ cup sugar
3 ½ teaspoons baking powder
1 teaspoon salt
1 cup maraschino cherries, coarsely chopped
1 cup walnuts, chopped

Add milk, egg and oil to the bread pan and set aside. Except for cherries and nuts, mix together remaining ingredients in a medium mixing bowl; add to bread pan. Now add cranberries and nuts. Select the Quick Bread setting and press Start.

CRANBERRY NUT BREAD

4 ounces orange juice
1 large egg
¼ cup butter or margarine
2 cups all-purpose flour
¾ cup sugar
1 tablespoon grated orange peel
1 ½ teaspoons baking powder
½ teaspoon baking soda
1 teaspoon salt
¾ cup cranberries, coarsely chopped
½ cup walnuts, chopped

Add orange juice, egg and butter to the bread pan and set aside. Except for cranberries and nuts, mix together remaining ingredients in a medium mixing bowl; add to bread pan. Now add cranberries and nuts. Select the Quick Bread setting and press Start.

DATE BREAD

6 ounces milk
4 tablespoons vegetable oil
2 large eggs
2 ½ cups all-purpose flour
1 cup white sugar
2 ½ teaspoons baking powder
½ teaspoon baking soda
1 teaspoon salt
¾ cup chopped dates

Add the ingredients to the bread maker in the order recommended by the manufacturer. Select the Quick Bread setting and press Start.

PUMPKIN SPICE NUTTY BREAD

1 cup canned or cooked and mashed pumpkin
1 cup sugar
⅓ cup oil
1 teaspoon vanilla extract
2 large eggs
1 ½ cups bread flour
2 teaspoons baking powder
¼ teaspoon salt
1 teaspoon ground cinnamon
½ teaspoon ground ginger
¼ teaspoon ground nutmeg
⅛ teaspoon ground cloves
⅔ cup chopped nuts

Add the ingredients to the bread maker in the order recommended by the manufacturer. Select the Quick Bread setting and press Start.

SWEET NUT BREAD

10 ounces milk
1 large egg
3 tablespoons vegetable oil
2 ½ cups all-purpose flour
⅓ cup white sugar
⅓ cup brown sugar, packed
3 ½ teaspoons baking powder
1 teaspoon salt
1 cup chopped nuts

Add milk, egg and oil to the bread pan and set aside. Mix together remaining ingredients in a medium mixing bowl; add to bread pan. Select the Quick Bread setting and press Start.

Sourdough Breads

Sourdough Starter

2 cups warm water
2 ¼ teaspoons active dry yeast
2 cups all-purpose flour

Place warm water and yeast in a glass bowl and stir. Let stand 10 minutes. Stir in flour and mix until a thick batter is formed. Cover with loosely with plastic wrap or a towel, or transfer to a wide mouth jar with a loose fitting lid. Place in a warm area for 24 hours. Stir flour mixture. Replace plastic wrap or loosely replace lid on jar. Return to warm area and let sit for 2 to 3 days until mixture bubbles and begins to smell sour. Stir and place in refrigerator.

Starter must be fed once a week and each time a portion is used in a recipe. To feed, remove 1 cup of starter and discard or give to a friend. To remaining starter, stir in 1 cup of all-purpose flour and 1 cup of warm water. Let sit, covered loosely, at room temperature 4-6 hours until bubbles form; return to refrigerator.

After removing a portion to use in a recipe, feed with equal amounts of all-purpose flour and warm water to equal the amount of starter removed. In other words, if 1 ¼ cups of starter is removed, replenish remaining starter with 1 ¼ cups of all-purpose flour and 1 ¼ cups of warm water. Stir, cover loosely and place in a warm area 4-6 hours until bubbles form. Return to refrigerator.

Always stir sourdough starter before removing a portion to use in a recipe.

BASIC SOURDOUGH BREAD

1 ¾ teaspoons active dry yeast
1 ½ teaspoons salt
1 ½ teaspoons sugar
2 ½ cups all-purpose flour
2 cups sourdough starter
3-5 ounces lukewarm water

Add the ingredients to the bread maker in the order recommended by the manufacturer. Select the Large Loaf/Light Crust or Large Loaf/Dark Crust setting and press Start.

CRUSTY SOURDOUGH BREAD

1 cup sourdough starter
4-5 ounces water
1 tablespoon vegetable shortening
3 cups bread flour
1 ½ teaspoons salt
2 tablespoons sugar
1 teaspoon bread machine (fast rise) yeast

Add the ingredients to the bread maker in the order recommended by the manufacturer. Select the Large Loaf/Light Crust setting and press Start.

SOURDOUGH BREAD LARGE LOAF

6-7 ounces water
1 ¼ cups sourdough starter
3 ½ cups bread flour
1 ½ teaspoons salt
1 ½ tablespoons sugar
2 teaspoons bread machine (fast rise) yeast

Add the ingredients to the bread maker in the order recommended by the manufacturer. Select the Large Loaf/Light Crust setting and press Start.

SOURDOUGH BREAD REGULAR LOAF

5 ounces water
1 cup sourdough starter
2 ¾ cups bread flour
1 teaspoons salt
1 tablespoons sugar
1 ½ teaspoons bread machine (fast rise) yeast

Add the ingredients to the bread maker in the order recommended by the manufacturer. Select the Regular Light setting and press Start.

SOURDOUGH PIZZA CRUST

1 cup sourdough starter
½ cup hot tap water
2 ½ cups all-purpose flour
1 teaspoon salt
½ teaspoon bread machine (fast rise) yeast

Add dough ingredients to your bread maker in the order recommended by the manufacturer. Select the Dough setting and press Start.

When cycle completes, divide dough into 2 equal sections and place on 2 greased 12-inch pizza pans. Cover with a towel and let rest for 15 minutes. Using your hands, press dough evenly toward the edges of the pans. Cover and let rest another 15 minutes. Press dough toward edges of pan again, if necessary.

Place in preheated 450° F oven and bake for 5 minutes. Remove from oven, cover with toppings and return to oven. Bake for an additional 8 to 10 minutes until toppings are done.

For thick crust pizza, use a single 14-inch pan and bake at 450° F 12 to 14 minutes during second bake time.

SOURDOUGH WHEAT LARGE LOAF

6 ounces water
1 ¼ cups sourdough starter
1 tablespoon molasses
1 ¾ cups bread flour
1 ¾ cups whole wheat flour
1 ½ teaspoons salt
2 teaspoon bread machine (fast rise) yeast

Add the ingredients to the bread maker in the order recommended by the manufacturer. Select the Large Loaf/Light Crust setting and press Start.

SOURDOUGH WHEAT REGULAR LOAF

6 ounces water
1 cup sourdough starter
1 tablespoon molasses
1 ½ cups bread flour
1 ½ cups whole wheat flour
1 teaspoons salt
1 ¾ teaspoons bread machine (fast rise) yeast

Add the ingredients to the bread maker in the order recommended by the manufacturer. Select the Regular Light setting and press Start.

ABOUT THE AUTHOR

Katherine Hupp is a native of West Virginia and lives in the rolling foothills of the Appalachian Mountains. She is a wife, mother and grandmother and enjoys country life.

She and her husband of 35 years are proud to have one fine son and two terrific grandsons.

Katherine spends much of her time gardening, cooking, canning and raising animals. Her hobbies include reading, writing, crocheting and stained glass.

Other books by Katherine Hupp for you to enjoy:

❖ Waffle Recipes: Wonderful Waffles and Syrups Cookbook
❖ Everything Zucchini Recipes Cookbook: Zucchini Breads, Muffins, Main Dishes, Desserts, Jams & Marmalade
❖ MUFFINS: 50 Appetizing Muffin Recipes with Nutritional Information
❖ Perfect Pie and Pastry Recipes: Homemade Dessert Pies Made Easy Cookbook
❖ Satisfying Slow Cooker Recipes: 41 Easy Crock Pot & Slow Cooker Dishes Cookbook
❖ Coconut Flour Low-Carb & Gluten Free Cookbook: 48 Tasty Recipes with Nutritional Information
❖ Zap-It! Microwave Cookbook 80 Quick & Easy Recipes
❖ Raising Backyard Chickens From Eggs To Egg Layers
❖ Names For Cats and Kittens: More Than 3000 Names For Male and Female Felines

Printed in Great Britain
by Amazon